B is for Babel

Author: Dr. C. White-Elliott

Illustrated by: Ariel

www.clfpublishing.org
909.315.3161

Illustrations by Ariel.

ISBN # 978-1-945102-45-5

Printed in the United States of America.

For

Aaron Palacios

my grandson

"Now the whole world had one language and a common speech. As people moved eastward, they found a plain in Shinar and settled there. They said to each other, 'Come, let's make bricks and bake them thoroughly.' They used brick instead of stone, and tar for mortar. The people began making bricks in their kilns."

Genesis 11:1-3

"Then they said, 'Come, let us build ourselves a city, with a tower that reaches to the heavens, so that we may make a name for ourselves; otherwise we will be scattered over the face of the whole earth'" (Genesis 11:4).

With the bricks they made, they began to lay the foundation of a great tower. The people worked together in peace.

Before long, the people had developed the

first layer of their tower. This motivated them

to continue working together to see the

project through to the end. They were

determined to reach heaven to see God.

Each day, the people worked long hours, looking forward to the completed tower. They continued to bake bricks and added on more and more layers. When they stood back to look at how much they had accomplished, they saw they were halfway done.

"Before long, they were almost done.

"But the LORD came down to see the city and the tower the people were building. The LORD said, 'If as one people speaking the same language they have begun to do this, then nothing they plan to do will be impossible for them.' When the Lord saw what the people were doing, He was unhappy. He had told the people to spread across the earth and to replenish it. Instead, they had stayed in one place and built a tower to go up to heaven."

Genesis 11:5-6

"Come, let us go down and confuse their language so they will not understand each other."

Genesis 11:7

The people who had spoken one language and were able to understand each other could no longer communicate. They could not understand what each other were saying.

"So the LORD scattered them from there over all the earth, and they stopped building the city."

(Genesis 11:8)

The people broke into groups. Only those who could speak the same language were together.

"That is why it was called Babel - because there the LORD confused the language of the whole world. From there the LORD scattered them over the face of the whole earth."

Genesis 11:9

From this event came many of the different languages of the world.

While on the surface it appears what the people were

doing was a wonderful thing, they were disobedient to

God. God told the people to spread across the earth and

replenish it. They decided to stay in one place and go up

to heaven instead of spreading out.

Remember, I Samuel 15:22b says,

"Behold, to obey is better than sacrifice."

God is our heavenly father. As His children,

we must obey God at all times!